A Rainy Day in Rochester

DATES IN THE STATES

A COUPLE TRAVELING THE UNITED
STATES ON A BUDGET

Mystery Date
Rochester, NY

By Dates in the States

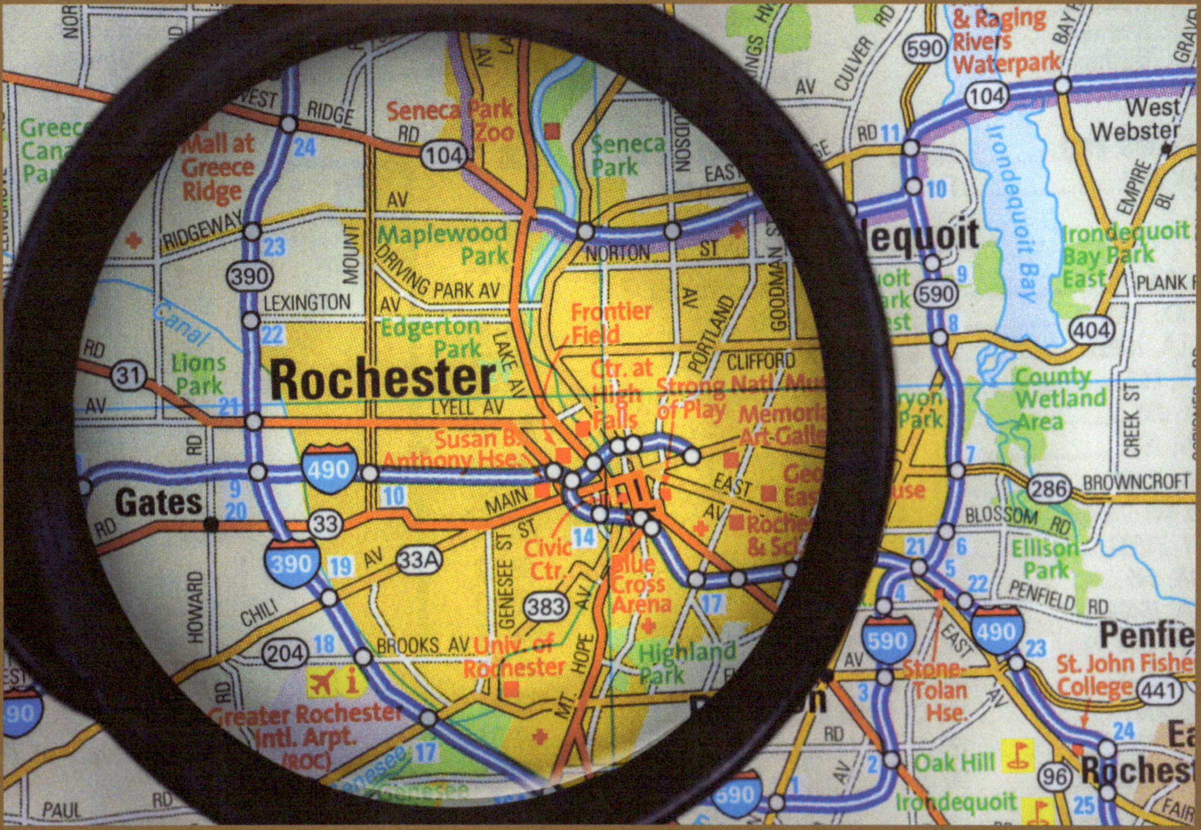

"Our passion is travel, and we want to share our adventures to inspire others to explore the world with their loved ones. Dare to live beyond the box."

Dates in the States

Introduction

Hey there! We're Crystal and Shane, the duo behind Dates in the States, where we share our love for discovering unique adventures, unforgettable moments, and hidden gems across the U.S. Whether you're searching for a fun date idea, a new place to explore, or just a little inspiration, we've got you covered!

Our Mystery Date Books are designed to help couples (and adventurous friends!) shake up their routine and experience the best local spots in a fun, intentional way. Inside, you'll find a curated collection of date ideas—each one meant to be completed over the course of a single day in a specific neighborhood. All of which are a surprise until you flip the page!

We hope this book helps you laugh more, explore more, and connect more—with each other and with your city. Let the mystery begin!

Here's What To Expect:

This Mystery Date was made for the kind of day when the skies are gray and the rain won't quit.

You'll start your day by getting creative at a scent studio, where you' blend your own custom candle or fragrance to take home. From there, head to a local winery for a relaxed tasting—sip, unwind, and forget about the weather. Wrap up the evening with a cozy dinner at one of our favorite hidden gems, where the food is as comforting as the atmosphere.

Rainy days don't have to mean staying in—this date is proof they can be some of the most memorable.

Start

Scents by Design

1312 University Avenue,
Rochester, NY 14607

Kick off your Mystery Date at Scents by Design, a charming boutique on University Avenue where the magic of scent comes alive. This candle-making bar invites you to craft your own hand-poured candles and premium home fragrances. Start by exploring their fragrance wall, filled with hundreds of scents to inspire you. Choose your favorite aromas and select a vessel for your creation—be it a jar, wax melts, or room spray.

With a drink in hand (yes, they serve alcohol!), you'll work with a scent specialist to blend your chosen fragrances. Whether you opt for a cozy winter blend or a fresh, summery mix, you'll have the chance to customize your scent to perfection. After crafting your unique fragrance, let your candles set while you move on to your next exciting destination.

2nd Stop
Living Roots
1252 University Avenue,
Rochester, NY 14607

Next, immerse yourself in the sophisticated charm of Living Roots Wine & Co. Enjoy one of their delicious wine flights featuring a curated selection of their finest wines, many of which are crafted at their location in Australia, bringing the land down under to The Flour City.

Pair your wines with a delectable charcuterie board, showcasing artisanal cheeses, cured meats, and gourmet accompaniments. The inviting atmosphere and expert guidance from their amazing staff create the perfect setting to relax, savor, and connect with your date.

Dessert Before Dinner?
We'll allow it!

After your wine tasting at Living Roots, treat yourselves to a little something sweet. Living Roots offers a rotating selection of desserts from Scratch Bakeshop, a local favorite (where we even got our wedding cake!). Be sure to try whatever delicious treat they have available at Living Roots, or if time allows, take a short walk over to Scratch Bakeshop and grab something to bring home for later—trust us, you'll be glad you did.

Scratch Bakeshop is known for their mouthwatering cookies, cakes, and other pastries, so it's a great way to extend the indulgence beyond just wine. You'll want to enjoy a treat either now or later, making this the perfect sweet spot between stops.

Final Stop
Carnegie Cellars

1168 Culver Road,
Rochester, NY 14609

End your evening at Carnegie Cellars, where an exceptional dinner awaits! This charming spot offers a delightful dining experience with a menu designed for sharing and savoring. The welcoming atmosphere and attentive service set the stage for a memorable meal. The owner's personal touch adds a special note, making each visit feel unique and warm.

For dinner, savor the delectable dishes, like the unforgettable pork belly bulgogi, complemented by pickled veggies that add a refreshing twist. The flavors are so captivating that you might forget to take photos! Enjoy a hearty meal and perhaps a little more wine as you wind down your romantic mystery date, creating lasting memories of a perfect evening.

DON'T FORGET!

Grab your candle from Scents by Design

Don't forget to grab your candle on the way home from your date! We know you started your adventure at Scent by Design, and typically they'll have you leave your candle while it sets. If it's before 8 p.m., make sure to swing by and pick up your custom creation on your way home. It's the perfect way to carry a piece of your date with you and enjoy the soothing scents you crafted together.

Add Your Photos

Keepsakes

Thank you for joining us on this mystery date adventure! We hope you've enjoyed the delightful experiences and memorable moments we've crafted just for you in Rochester, NY.

But the adventure doesn't stop here! Keep exploring exciting myster dates in other cities and uncover new romantic experiences across the U.S. by visiting our website, DatesInTheStates.com. There, you can purchase both physical copies and digital downloads of our mystery date books. Plus, don't miss out on our Mystery Date Book Club, where you can receive a brand-new mystery date book every month!

Tag us in your date photos on social media! @datesinthestates

Check out some of our other Mystery Date Books:

Webster, NY – Lakeside charm, local eats, and small-town surprises perfect for a relaxing day out.

Haunted Irondequoit, NY – Explore the eerie side of town with this chilling look into the most haunted businesses and their spine-tingling stories.

Hornell, NY – A hidden gem in the Finger Lakes region with art, nature, and charming local spots waiting to be discovered.

I Love ROC + Cats – Explore local art, sip coffee with adoptable cats, browse a charming bookstore, and end with a delicious downtown meal. Perfect for solo dates, friend hangouts, or cat-loving couples!

✉ Shop them all at DatesInTheStates.com
📷 Tag your adventures: @datesinthestates

Your next date is only a page away.

About the Creators

Crystal, the writer and creator, is a storyteller at heart. When she's not uncovering hidden gems for the next date night idea, she runs her own digital marketing company, helping small businesses improve their content marketing, increase visibility in their communities, and streamline their online presence.
Visit: crystalstatskey.com

Shane, her husband and partner in adventure, is a dedicated personal trainer and the owner of Beekstar Fitness in Irondequoit, NY. He specializes in working with clients who have limited mobility, helping them build muscle and focus on pain areas so they can regain strength and confidence in their daily lives.
Visit: beekstarfitness.com

Crystal and Shane have explored every U.S. state except Alaska (coming soon!) and are now visiting countries in alphabetical order. Whether road-tripping or curating Mystery Date experiences, they' always chasing their next adventure.

Local Love

A few local gems in Rochester worth exploring on your next date.

MEMORIAL ART GALLERY (MAG)

ART MUSEUM

500 UNIVERSITY AVE, ROCHESTER, NY 14607

ROCHESTER BRAINERY

FUN CLASSES TO TAKE TOGETHER

176 ANDERSON AVE F109, ROCHESTER, NY 14607

ARTISANWORKS

OFF BEAT MUSEUM

565 BLOSSOM RD # L, ROCHESTER, NY 14610

Want to see your business here? See the next page for details on how to join!

Want to be featured?

MYSTERY DATE BOOK PACKAGES

—

Are you a small business looking to reach new customers? Feature your business in our next Mystery Date Book! Choose from our partnership packages below to connect with couples seeking unique experiences and exclusive deals.

Package One

LOCAL LOVE LISTING

—

A quick shoutout to show you're part of the neighborhood vibe.

Listed in the "Local Love" section of your designated neighborhood date book

Includes business name, address, and social link

Optional: Offer a small promo (e.g., 10% off for book holders)

1 social media shout-out when the book launches

$45

Package Two

FEATURE STOP

—

You're not just a business— you're part of the experience.

Marked as a "Must-Stop" on a Mystery Date

Full-page feature in the book with your story, offerings and photo

Includes 1 social media feature — a dedicated post and story highlighting your business

Note: To ensure each feature is genuine and experience-based, we require a hosted visit prior to inclusion.

$95

Package Three

PARTNER & SELLER

—

Be the spot and the source.

Everything in Tier 2

PLUS: Option to sell the Mystery Date Books at your location

Includes a bulk purchase of 10 books (yours to price + sell)

Keep 100% of the profits from in-store sales

Bonus: Tag as an official pickup location in our promotions

$150

Prices are subject to change

Feel free to reach us at any time by sending us an email to say hi and to learn more! We look forward to hearing from you.

| www.datesinthestates.com | datesinthestatesblog@gmail.com |

Sponsors & Affiliates

Our sponsors and affiliates help make our adventures possible! Explore the amazing brands and businesses that support our community.

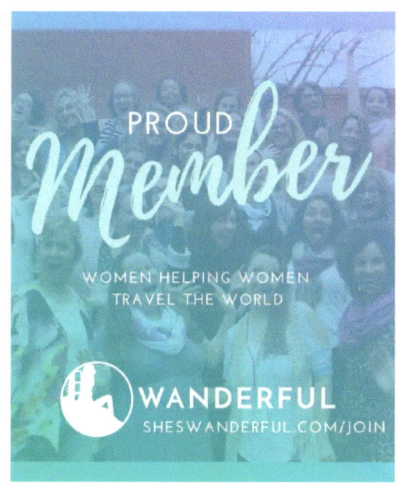

Wanderful

Wanderful is a global community for women who love to travel. Connect, explore, and join a local hub near you!

Join our Book Club!

Join our Mystery Date Book Club and be part of a travel-inspired community, discovering unique local adventures together!

HomeExchange

HomeExchange lets you swap homes with travelers worldwide for authentic, affordable stays. Join today and travel differently!

Shop our books at a store near you!

Little Button Craft
658 South Ave.
Rochester, NY 14620

The Pawsitive Cat Cafe
120 East Ave. Ste 100
Rochester, NY 14604

Yesterday's Muse Books
32 West Main St.
Webster, NY 14580

Writers & Books
740 University Ave,
Rochester, NY 14607

Littleberger Florist
63 North Avenue,
Webster, NY 14580

Flight Wine Bar
262 Exchange Blvd,
Rochester, NY 14608

Scents by Design
728 University Ave,
Rochester, NY 14607

Union Tavern
4565 Culver Rd,
Irondequoit, NY 14622

DATES IN THE STATES

A COUPLE TRAVELING THE UNITED
STATES ON A BUDGET

Contact Us

datesinthestates.com

datesinthestatesblog@gmail.com

Based in Rochester, NY

CONNECT WITH US ON SOCIAL!

@DATESINTHESTATES

_____

www.ingramcontent.com/pod-product-compliance
Lightning Source LLC
Chambersburg PA
CBHW041622120626

46551CB00003B/544